Guinea Pig

A guide to selection, housing, care,
nutrition, behaviour, health, breeding,
species and colours

about pets

Contents

Contents

Foreword

The book you're holding has been written to give you the basic information you need to start keeping Guinea Pigs as pets. Apart from that, it offers you some background information and some facts worth knowing. Guinea Pigs are popular pets and are tame and robust, but they do have specific needs in feeding and care.

Apart from general information about origins, history, buying, feeding, housing, reproduction and health, some attention is paid to the hobby of keeping and breeding small animals. A separate chapter is devoted to special Guinea Pigs. These are Guinea Pigs that are possibly related to the tame Guinea Pig and include some varieties kept as pets by experienced enthusiasts.

About Pets

© 2009 About Pets bv
P.O. Box 26, 9989 ZG Warffum,
the Netherlands
www.aboutpets.info
E-mail: management@aboutpets.info

ISBN: 9781852792145

First printing September 2003
Second printing May 2005
Third revised printing 2006
Fourth printing 2009

Photos: About Pets photography team

Acknowledgements:
Photos: Dick Hamer and Rob Doolaard

The Guinea Pig, also known as the Cavy, is one of the most popular children's pets, but even adults can get a lot of pleasure out of keeping and breeding this little animal. Guinea Pigs are exceptionally friendly animals and are rarely aggressive.

A Guinea Pig that bites is a real exception. They're also ideally sized, not too big (easy for children to handle) and not too small (they can weather handling by occasionally perhaps rather too-enthusiastic children).
A Guinea Pig is an animal without excessive demands in terms of care or feeding, but you do have to observe a few rules to avoid problems. They need to be fed with care; a poorly balanced diet can quickly make a Guinea Pig seriously ill.

Origins

Long before the Spanish conquered South America, Guinea Pigs were kept as pets in Peru and Chile.
The Incas bred Guinea Pigs mainly for their meat and fur. The meat (which apparently tastes similar to suckling pig) was regarded as a special delicacy and was eaten at feasts and weddings. These animals probably also played a role in this highly civilised people's religious ceremonies. Mummified Guinea Pigs have been found in Inca tombs.

At the end of the sixteenth century, Spanish explorers and Dutch seafarers brought the Guinea Pig to Europe via Guinea on the coast of West Africa, presumably to provide fresh meat during the long voyage. However, a number of animals escaped the frying pan and made it to Europe alive. The Guinea Pig was already known in Europe at the time, because it had been described and illustrated by the Swiss biologist Gessner in 1533. It would still be a long time before the Guinea Pig became the popular pet it is today, but Guinea Pigs are known to have been traded by the Dutch in France and England in 1680. They were at first so expensive that only the rich could afford to buy them as a curiosity or as a playmate for their children. Particularly in Britain, Guinea Pig lovers worked hard to make the animal better known, but it would take until after World War II before they became really popular. A spin-off was that they were increasingly used as subjects for medical experiments (guinea pigs!) in laboratories, and they played an important role in the fight against tuberculosis and the development of a serum against diphtheria.

In the wild

Many varieties of Guinea Pig (and other Cavy types) still live in the wild in South America.
They belong to the rodent order (*Rodentia*). Rodents form the largest group of mammals; of all the mammals in the world, more than half are rodents. The rodent order comprises more than three hundred families and almost three thousand varieties. The chart on the next page clearly shows what place the Cavies occupy in the mammal hierarchy. The Cavy types that live in the wild range widely in terms of size and weight. The smallest weigh some 200 g, the largest up to 70 kg. In length they range from 15 cm to 1.3 m, but they all have some characteristics in common. Relative to their body, their head is large, and they all have four toes on their front paws with relatively wide, curved nails. They are all digitigrades (i.e., they walk on their toes) with many similarities in terms of gait. In contrast to other rodents, normal Guinea Pigs cannot climb or stand on their back legs. They also don't use their front paws to hold their food. In their countries of origin guinea pigs are not exactly rare. They have virtually no economic value for man, so they're not hunted in great numbers. The most common variety is the wild Guinea Pig (*Cavia aperea*). Some experts believe our 'tame' Guinea Pig is a descendant of this variety, while others give this honour to the Wild Cavy (*Cavia aperea tschudi*). In the chapter 'Other species' you can read more about these wild varieties.

Confusing name

Why the Guinea Pig is called a pig is a bit of a riddle? There is some

The largest cavy type: the Capybara

A Guinea Pig and a Degu

A wild Guinea Pig

In general

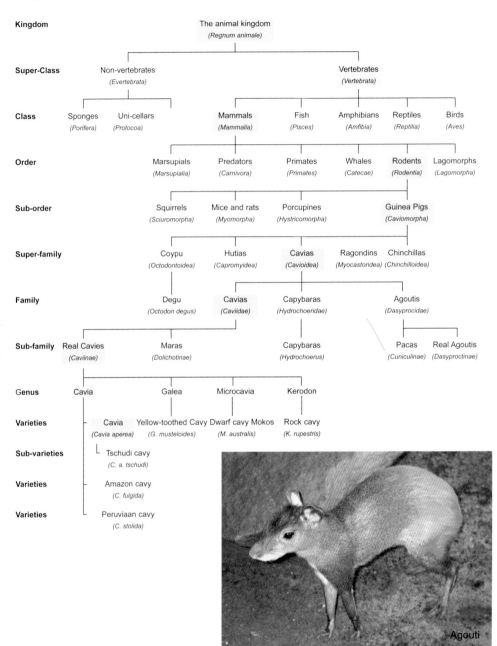

Kingdom			The animal kingdom *(Regnum animale)*			
Super-Class		Non-vertebrates *(Evertebrata)*		Vertebrates *(Vertebrata)*		
Class	Sponges *(Porifera)*	Uni-cellars *(Protocoa)*	**Mammals** *(Mammalia)*	Fish *(Pisces)* — Amphibians *(Amfibia)* — Reptiles *(Reptilia)* — Birds *(Aves)*		
Order			Marsupials *(Marsupialia)* — Predators *(Carnivora)* — Primates *(Primates)* — Whales *(Catecae)* — **Rodents** *(Rodentia)* — Lagomorphs *(Lagomorpha)*			
Sub-order			Squirrels *(Sciuromorpha)* — Mice and rats *(Myomorpha)* — Porcupines *(Hystricomorpha)* — Guinea Pigs *(Caviomorpha)*			
Super-family			Coypu *(Octodontoidea)* — Hutias *(Capromyidea)* — Cavias *(Cavioidea)* — Ragondins *(Myocastoridea)* — Chinchillas *(Chinchilloidea)*			
Family			Degu *(Octodon degus)* — Cavias *(Caviidae)* — Capybaras *(Hydrochoeridae)* — Agoutis *(Dasyprocidae)*			
Sub-family	Real Cavies *(Caviinae)*	Maras *(Dolichotinae)*	Capybaras *(Hydrochoerus)*	Pacas *(Cuniculinae)* — Real Agoutis *(Dasyproctinae)*		
Genus	Cavia	Galea	Microcavia	Kerodon		
Varieties	Cavia *(Cavia aperea)*	Yellow-toothed Cavy *(G. musteloides)*	Dwarf cavy Mokos *(M. australis)*	Rock cavy *(K. rupestris)*		
Sub-varieties	Tschudi cavy *(C. a. tschudi)*					
Varieties	Amazon cavy *(C. fulgida)*					
Varieties	Peruviaan cavy *(C. stolida)*					

Agouti

speculation that it may have been confused with the American ground hog, and while its French name is Cochon d'Inde (Indies Pig) and the English know it as Guinea Pig, the one thing that's clear is that it isn't a pig. Still, all these names have that notion in common, and the male is indeed known as a 'boar' and the female as a 'sow'! The only correct name is, in fact, 'Cavy' which is also commonly used in the United States of America.

Green acouchi

Capybara

Mara

Buying a pet is a different matter to buying a toy or a pound of sugar. An animal is a living creature and we need to treat it well and responsibly. Whether we buy a dog, a cat, a goldfish or a Guinea Pig – we are their custodians, and we accept responsibility for their wellbeing when we buy them.

If we don't care for them, they may fall ill, and if we don't give them a proper home they can escape and, sadly, all too often meet with death in the wild. The care of one animal may take (much) more time than that of another, but it has to be part of one's daily routine, regardless.

Whenever you consider buying a pet, get all the information you need before you buy. Is this the right animal for your family situation? How much care does it need, and do you have the time for it over the long term? What does the animal eat, what kind of cage does it need, does it live alone or is it better to have a pair, or a group even? How much will it cost to buy and look after (including vet's bills) and can you afford that? Get the answers to these questions to avoid disappointment and problems later. If you're in any doubt, don't buy the animal!

Before you take your Guinea Pig home, you must prepare proper accommodation for it there. After all, you can't keep a rodent in a cardboard box forever.

If you're buying a Guinea Pig for a child, it's important to agree

beforehand who is going to feed it and keep its home clean. Experience shows that children often promise a lot in their initial enthusiasm, but don't always keep them when faced with the chores over the longer term. Remember too, that a pet needs care whilst you're on holidays or otherwise away from home. The same applies, by the way, when you come home tired after a long day at work or school.

All in all, caring for a pet usually brings lots of pleasure. It's like having a little piece of nature in your home, and Guinea Pigs make excellent pets. They are quiet and calm animals and it's rare for them to bite or scratch, which makes them excellent company for children. Their robustness makes them suitable for younger children, and they can even take a knock or two at the hands of a toddler.

One or more

Guinea Pigs are group or family animals by nature. They feel happiest in the company of their own kind. You can keep a Guinea Pig by itself, but then you must give it plenty of attention. If it doesn't get this attention, it will slowly but surely waste away.

A Guinea Pig can also live well with a small or medium-sized rabbit. However, don't put several adult males together in one home: they won't accept each other.

Where to buy

Most Guinea Pigs are sold through pet shops. Most pet shop owners know what care the animals they sell need, but there are always some unfortunate exceptions. Often, it's easy to spot what kind of shop you're dealing with. Are the cages clean? Do all the animals have clean water? Do they look fit and healthy? It is also important that you get complete and honest information about the animal.

Most pet shops buy their animals from amateur or professional breeders. These try to breed 'perfect' individuals, often guided by show standards.

If their Guinea Pigs do not meet the strict show competition rules, they are selected at a young age to be sold. These animals are usually perfectly healthy, but may not be quite the right colour, or they may have a spot of colour in the wrong place.

Another type of breeder also exists. They try to breed as many animals they can in the shortest possible time, to earn a fast buck. They pay little or no attention to the animals' health and aren't worried about hygiene or in-breeding. Moreover, many of the young are separated from their mother at far too young an age. If you want a good breeder, get in touch with your local animal shelter, small-animal club, or the RSPCA.

You can also buy a Guinea Pig at an animal show. It is well worth visiting such shows even if you're not (yet) looking to buy a Guinea Pig.

Transport

When you buy a Guinea Pig, you have to get the animal home. This is often done in a cardboard box, but this is not the best solution. It would not be the first time (and won't be the last time either) that a Guinea Pig gnaws a hole in such a box and goes off on a journey of discovery in shopping bag or car. So it's best to get a proper travel cage in anticipation – you can buy them at any pet shop. Make sure it provides proper protection and ventilation. Never leave the travel container with the animal in a car

parked in the sun. The resulting (very) high temperature may be fatal for your animal.

Things to check

If you're planning to buy a Guinea Pig, pay attention to the following points:

- The animal must be healthy. A healthy Guinea Pig has clear, bright eyes and is lively. Its genital areas must be clean, and the animal should have no wounds, suspicious swellings, scale or scabs. The nose, ears and lips must be clean and dry and not crusted. The coat should be smooth and glossy (except for the shorthaired varieties).
- The Guinea Pig should be well fed, but not fat. It should feel solid and should not display a high back or sunken flanks.
- Check its breathing. Squeaky or

wheezing breathing may point to an infection. Droppings must be dry and firm. Wet, soft droppings can be a sign of intestinal infection.

- Your Guinea Pig should not be too young or too small. During the first few weeks of its life, the young animal gets antibodies from its mother's milk, which it badly needs. Ask the seller the animal's age. Never buy a Guinea Pig younger than five weeks, or one that seems far too light for its age.

- Nor should your Guinea Pig be too old. Older animals die sooner, of course, but they also find it more difficult to get used to new surroundings. You can tell the older animals by their coat, which is less glossy and may have some bald patches.

- Also check the other animals that share the cage with the one of your choice. Even if the one you want seems healthy, if any of its cage-mates are sick, your new pride and joy may also be carrying an infection.

- Check whether your Guinea Pig is really the sex the vendor says it is. This is an area where mistakes frequently occur, leading to situation where two 'females' suddenly start to produce young. Adult boars are recognised by their testicles. On younger animals, an experienced breeder or enthusiast can verify gender by carefully pressing out the penis.

Rodents are often fed the same food day-in day-out for years: mixed rodent food.

However, research into the feeding habits of rodents in the wild has shown that they generally need a different, much more varied diet.

Vitamin C

Feeding a Guinea Pig takes a lot of care. If you feed your Guinea Pig mixed rodent food every day, you can rely on it that the animal will become ill. Just like humans and the apes, a Guinea Pig does not produce its own vitamin C. It must get it every day in its food. A fully-grown Guinea Pig needs about 20 mg of vitamin C per day to stay healthy. Growing or pregnant Guinea Pigs need double that amount.

A vitamin C deficiency manifests itself in intestinal problems, growth disorders, reduced fertility, regular colds – and death of young animals.

There are various ways to meet this important vitamin C requirement. The most natural way is to feed the animal green vegetables with a high vitamin C content, but then you have to do that every day.

To avoid the risk that you may forget to give it its greens, choose a commercial food that contains enough vitamin C. Mixed rodent or rabbit food, or other grain mixes, often contain insufficient vitamin C or none at all. The accompanying table gives an overview of well-known Guinea Pig foods. Remember that there is usually

Feeding

Vitamin C in vegetables and fruit (in mg per 100 g)	
Carrots	5 mg
Endives	10 mg
Apple	10 mg
Tomato	20 mg
Blanched celery	25 mg
Orange	50 mg
Cauliflower	75 mg
Broccoli	110 mg
Chicory	115 mg
Kale	125 mg
Sprouts	150 mg
Paprika	150 mg
Parsley	170 mg
Rose-hip	500 mg

The table gives you an overview of a number of vegetable and fruit varieties with the vitamin C content per 100 g.

vitamin C in the pressed (grass) pellets. If you give a Guinea Pig too much food, it will pick out what it likes best and leave the rest, which may just be those all-important vitamin pellets. Only give a Guinea Pig more food when it has completely finished its previous meal.

Dry foods

Dry food is a collective name for any food that is not fresh: loose grain types, mixed grain with grass kernels and ready-made pellets. You can buy maize, grain, barley, yeast, millet and various seeds from seed merchants. However, it's not worth the effort mixing your Guinea Pig's food yourself. Apart from that, such mixes contain no vitamin C. Off-the-shelf Guinea Pig grain mixtures contain everything your animal needs for a balanced

diet. These mixed foods also contain grass pellets. Experience shows that Guinea Pigs eat these pellets last, so it's important that they get precisely the amount of food that they eat in one day. Only give them additional food when their bowl is empty.

There are also ready-made pellets in the shops. These pellets are all identical in their composition. They contain all the necessary nutrients and provide a perfect diet, without having to find and wash green vegetables. Still, apart from their ease of use, it must be pretty boring for the Guinea Pig to have to eat the same food every day. Seed and grains have a high

nutritional value. A Guinea Pig that gets too much mixed grain and too little green food and exercise can get fat quickly. Then it's important to give it less food and to make sure it gets more exercise. Whichever food you choose, always make a note of the use-by date. Food that is older than three months loses a large portion of its nutritional value.

Green foods
In the wild, Guinea Pigs eat more green food than grains, so green food must also make up a substantial part of a pet Guinea Pig's diet. Here we mean those green foods that are suitable for a Guinea Pig. This list is almost

inexhaustible, but don't take a risk when in doubt. Only give your Guinea Pig things you're sure it can eat. You can find wild herbs in the bush and fields. Don't collect green food for your pet from the side of roads or in areas with heavy industry, as such plants are probably contaminated with lead and other poisons. Also avoid agricultural land, because of insecticides. To avoid any risk, wash any green food thoroughly, then let it drain and dry a little. You can give your Guinea Pig practically any fruit or vegetable, although some cabbage varieties can cause intestinal problems. Greenhouse lettuce contains a lot of nitrate, so limit cabbage and lettuce to small quantities only.

Hay

Hay is an important element in a healthy diet for Guinea Pigs. Although it contains little in terms of nutrients, it's indispensable for the digestion. A Guinea Pig must have fresh hay available every day. Apart from the important fibre, it also contains calcium and magnesium. You can buy a bale of hay from a farmer or seed merchant, or in smaller packages from pet shops.

Good, fresh hay contains young grass, clover and herbs. It is dry, but still a little green and has a wonderful smell. Poor quality hay contains practically no herbs, because it's often taken from barren meadows. You can recognise old hay by its yellowish colour. It also gives off dust, which can be especially harmful to your animal's bronchial tracts. Apart from that, old hay no longer contains nutrients.

Water

That Guinea Pigs only need a little to drink is a fable. Even if you give them plenty of green food, they still need fresh water every day. Give them water at room temperature from a drinking bottle. Clean the bottle regularly, as poisonous algae can build up in it. Guinea Pigs sometimes have the habit of drinking from their bottle with a mouth full of food, so it can become dirty or blocked. Check the bottle and replace the water every day.

Vitamins and minerals

With a well-balanced diet, you won't need to add any supplements to the drinking water, but sick animals and suckling mothers do need some extra vitamin C, which you can add in the form of 50 mg tablets. Most Guinea Pigs like them so much they will happily take them from your hand, but don't use them as snacks. Too much vitamin C can also be harmful.

You can also hang a so-called 'mineral-lick' in the cage. If they need extra salt or minerals they can get them by licking at it.

Hay with herbs

Snacks and extras

A Guinea Pig is a real rodent. To keep its teeth in good condition it needs something to gnaw on. There are various munchies available in pet shops, but you can also use branches or twigs from willow, fruit or other deciduous trees. Hard bits of dried bread or some crispbread are also suitable snacks.

Don't give a Guinea Pig crisps, biscuits, sweets or sugar lumps as extras. These are extremely unhealthy for pets, as they contain too much salt, sugar and fat. There are enough healthy snacks you can use to give your Guinea Pig a treat.

Of course, different animals have different tastes; one Guinea Pig may like something that another won't touch, but parsley, chicory, carrot leaves, rose-hips and kiwis will usually bring a smile to their faces.

If you want to keep a Guinea Pig responsibly and give it a comfortable home, it's important to take a look at how they live in the wild.

Even if your Guinea Pig lives in a hutch or a cage at home, it is still possible to get close to their natural living conditions, making the animal feel as comfortable as possible.

In the wild

The tame Guinea Pig that we keep as a pet does not exist in the wild. A possible ancestor, the wild Guinea Pig, is found in large numbers in South America. The indigenous population has kept it in semi-captivity for centuries. Even today, countless Guinea Pigs live in and around villages where, close to mankind, they rummage around for food.

The Tschudi Cavy, another candidate for ancestor of our pet Guinea Pig, tends to live closer to nature. It is found mostly in mountainous areas up to 4200 metres high.

Various wild varieties of Cavia live in mountains, on savannahs, and in swamps, but they tend to avoid the lush tropical rain forests. They live in burrows, in groups of five to ten animals. They prefer to use existing, natural cavities or burrows that other animals have dug. If there aren't any available, they get to work themselves. Cavy burrow systems are not complex or deep. They only serve as a hideaway and nest.

Housing in captivity

Guinea Pigs are not overly fussy about their home. They feel more

comfortable if they live together with Guinea Pigs, but it's not a good idea to keep two boars together if there are also sows around. The males will certainly get into fights should this be the case.

A good Guinea Pig home must first be dry and draught-free, but also well ventilated. Draughts and damp are the biggest threats to your Guinea Pig's health.

The same as with other pets, 'the bigger the better' rule also applies to your Guinea Pig's home. The minimum size for a single Guinea Pig is a cage of 60 x 40 cm. If you keep two or more together, the cage must be proportionally bigger, of course.

Types of cage

The simplest and quickest way to find out what cages are available, is to pay a visit to the pet shop. There you'll find Guinea Pig cages in all shapes and sizes. They mostly consist of a plastic base with metal wire top. Make sure the sides of the base are high enough to prevent your Guinea Pig from throwing hay and wood shavings out of the cage.

If you're a moderately skilled DIY person, you can even make a cage yourself. That way you can build it exactly as you want it, and make it to the size that suits your situation.

In principle, the cage does not need a lid. Guinea Pigs cannot climb or jump so they won't try to escape. But if you have a cat, a dog, a ferret or some other beast of prey in the house, then a lid is indicated.

Don't keep a Guinea Pig with mice, hamsters or rats in the same cage; it only gets on well with a rabbit. If you build the cage yourself, put in a second 'floor'. This should not be higher than 15 cm and you will need to build a ladder leading up to it. The space under this floor will then serve as a hideaway.

Old aquarium or glass containers are unsuitable for Guinea Pigs because of the lack of ventilation.

Guinea Pigs inside

A Guinea Pig can happily live inside the whole year round; you'll establish good contact, and your animal will be much tamer. A Guinea Pig is a social animal and will frequently announce its presence with its infectious squeaks. If you do keep a Guinea Pig in an indoor cage (usually small), you must let it run around somewhere in the house at least once a day.

Guinea Pigs outside

If you want to let your Guinea Pig enjoy some fresh air, the easiest way is to put it in a cage in the garden or on the balcony. Only do

Housing

You can also keep a Guinea Pig outdoors on a more permanent basis, but you must bring it inside when the daytime temperature is below fifteen degrees (mainly in winter, depending on where you live). A run with a covered section or a rabbit hutch is ideal. It must be absolutely frost-free, preferably a double-walled hutch with plenty of hay. In the wild, Cavies also live in the mountains and can handle the cold. But after centuries of domestication, the tame Guinea Pig has changed so much that it can no longer deal with the cold.

An outdoor run is ideal for Guinea Pigs, but must be free from frost.

this in good weather in spring or summer. Make sure there's plenty of protection from sun and rain. It's important not to take a Guinea Pig directly from a heated room into the cool outside air (or vice versa). Big temperature variations are bad for its health.

Remember that outdoor cages are very attractive to rats, mice and other unwanted guests, but a properly built run of durable materials will keep them out. Rotting parts of an outdoor hutch can harbour mould, insects and other pests, so keep it well maintained.

One disadvantage of an outdoor home is that you have a lot less contact with your pet(s). A single Guinea Pig will have hard time when kept outdoors by itself. Experience also shows that Guinea Pigs that are kept indoors live substantially longer than 'outdoor' Guinea Pigs. Finally, it is not recommended to keep longhaired Guinea Pigs outside.

Cage litter

For a long time, wood shavings were used in pet cages. Often

Some rules for a DIY hutch:
- Use a hard material for the floor so that urine or water can't soak in (metal, glass or plasticised panels are best).
- Don't use materials that can splinter if gnawed at.
- Don't use plasticised wire netting.
- Don't use wire netting as a floor.
- The cage should get enough light.
- The cage should not stand in the full sun, especially in summer.
- The cage should be easy to clean.
- Make sure there's good ventilation, but definitely no draughts.
- Humidity must be neither too high, nor too low..

Hay with herbs

Luxury bedding

Schredded paper

Wood shavings

referred to as sawdust, they were actually shavings. They absorb moisture exceptionally well and hardly smell, but a disadvantage is that they usually contain a lot of dust. Research in recent years has shown that this dust can be a serious problem for rodents. There are now many other types of cage litter on the market that are less harmful for animals.

Wood shavings
As stated above, shavings are no longer regarded as suitable cage litter. Most pets (including Guinea Pigs) get the dust into their lungs and, over time, this can cause inflammation. Now that the dust problem has been generally recognised, some types of shavings are being cleaned more thoroughly by the manufacturers.

Hay
Guinea Pigs like to use hay as nesting material; they also like to chew on it. It is an important part of their diet. Hay, however, does not absorb moisture well, which makes it not really suitable as cage litter.

Straw
Straw is much too coarse to be suitable as cage litter or nest material for Guinea Pigs. There is a product on the market, which is made of shredded straw and is wonderfully soft and ideal as nesting material. However, it absorbs too little moisture to be suitable as cage litter.

Cat litter
There are many, many different kinds of cat litter on the market. Some are suitable to keep Guinea Pigs or other rodents on, especially those made from maize. These absorb plenty of moisture and do good service. Cat litter made of stone or clay grit is less suitable, mainly because it tends to be dusty.

Pressed pellets
In recent years various cage litters have appeared on the market that

consist of pressed pellets. Some have sharp edges which wouldn't be very comfortable for the animal.

Sand
Sand absorbs too little moisture to be used as cage litter. Apart from that, it gets dirty.

Shredded paper
There are also various types of shredded-paper-based litters on offer. These shreds are ideal to

play with and can be used as nest material. But they absorb much too little moisture to be useful as cage litter. Never make cage litter yourself from old newspapers. The printing ink can poison your Guinea Pig.
In conclusion, use a cage litter that easily absorbs moisture, in combination with a soft, insulating nesting material.

Interior
A cage with only cage litter and nothing else is a very barren home. A Guinea Pig cage should also be fitted with a hay manger, which you can buy at a pet shop. Water should be given in a drinking bottle that you hang on the outside, with the spout pointing into the cage. There are two small steel balls in the spout and by moving these the Guinea Pig gets water. Any Guinea Pig will quickly get used to a drinking bottle.
Use a heavy stone dish for dry food. Guinea Pigs like to stand at the dish with their forepaws on the edge. A dish that is too light will easily tip over. Green food can simply be laid on the cage floor.

Burrowers by nature, Guinea Pigs like hideaways. This can be a little wooden hut or box for them to creep into when they need peace and quiet. If their cage is regularly taken outside, their hideaway should not have a black or dark-coloured roof, or it will get too hot in the sun.

Guinea Pigs are clean animals that will select their own toilet corner. Clean this corner every couple of days, then you will only need to clean out the whole cage every other week or so.

Dangers

A pet that is reasonably tame and kept in a smallish cage needs to be let out regularly for a run. Sufficient exercise is very important for an animal's health. If you let your Guinea Pig run in the house, garden or on the balcony, you need to be aware of some dangers.

Watch out for electrical cords and cables. A Guinea Pig will gnaw at anything and they're not equipped to handle 220 volts. Make sure you don't step on your Guinea Pig and that it doesn't get caught in the door. (That may sound exaggerated, but it's happened!). Watch other pets carefully (dog or cat). Pot plants can be poisonous for a Guinea Pig, so make sure it can't get at them. Don't let it run on a table or high edge; it is a poor judge of heights and could seriously injure itself in a fall.

Make sure your garden or balcony is properly fenced off. A Guinea Pig will quickly find any hole, and your neighbour's dog may not be expecting company. Guinea Pigs are no longer used to bushes and shrubs. They can easily be injured by spikes and thorns. Finally, don't let your Guinea Pig get wet in the rain; wet and exposed to the wind, a Guinea Pig can become ill in no time at all.

Many people breed Guinea Pigs as a hobby. They take them to small-animal shows, where they hope to win prizes with their finest examples.

The Guinea Pig's appearance, colour and coat are subject to strict rules; not everything is permitted. The perfect Guinea Pig fulfils the standards of the breeders' association.

The Standard

The breeders' association standard describes how Guinea Pigs and other small rodents such as the Rabbit, the Golden Hamster, the Mongolian Gerbil and the tame rat or fancy mouse should ideally look. An animal entered for a competition can earn points in seven categories. In the table you can see how many points a Guinea Pig can score in each category. Points are deducted for any defects depending on their seriousness. The animal that finally scores the most points is the winner and earns the title 'best in show'.

Guinea Pigs come in many more colourings and markings than those included in the standard. But a colouring or marking is only officially recognised if it's in the standard. For example: red and gold Guinea Pigs are described in the standard. If a Guinea Pig is entered that is neither red (a warm maroon colour) nor gold (a warm orange colour) but something in-between, then it doesn't meet the requirements and will get a medium or poor score in the 'colour' category.

One can view the animal as a 'poor' red or gold Guinea Pig. It is also possible to enter the animal as a 'new colour' for the standard, but not every mixture of two colours will automatically be approved. There are a number of requirements that a colour or marking must meet to be included. At least four animals with the new colour or marking must be entered for the federation's show. There they are judged and possibly approved by the standards committee of the association. The first step is preliminary recognition. If, after three years, there are enough animals with the new colour or marking, it is then fully recognised.

The Judging

During judging, the animals entered are judged on the following points:

Type and build

This part of the standard describes a Guinea Pig's build. 'A Guinea Pig should make a strong and muscular impression, which is expressed mainly by an attractively developed wide head, short powerful neck and the main characteristic of the animal: its high, wide and muscular shoulder and a well-filled chest and ribcage underline its build, which should be powerful, short and compact.'

Weight

Guinea Pigs can be entered for shows in two categories, young or adult. This age category is taken into account when judging an animal's weight. According to the standard, a Guinea Pig should be large, but not coarse, ponderous or fat. Its weight may vary between 900 and 1200 grams.

Coat and hair condition

This part of the standard varies per variety and hair structure. A number of different hair structures are recognised for the Guinea Pig. The most common is the normal-haired Guinea Pig. This has a close, soft and glossy coat with fine hairs and coarser topcoat hairs. Hairs are approximately 3 cm long. There are also Rex,

Silver agouti

Gold

Satin crème

Points awarded for Guinea Pigs

Type and build	20	points
Size	10	points
Hair and coat condition	20	points
Head, eyes and ears	15	points
Top and belly colour	15	points
Base colour	15	points
Body condition	5	points
Total	100	points

Chocolate

Red crested

Crème

Crested (Coronet) and Shorthaired Guinea Pigs, Shelties and Peruvians. See also the following chapter on *Breeds*.

Head and ears
This section is also described per variety and markings. You can find more details in the following chapter.

Topcoat and belly colour
The topcoat is understood to be the surface colour on the animal's back. The word 'surface' is very important here. A hair usually consists of different colours. The base of a hair (at the body) will have a certain colour, the base colour. In certain cases the intermediate part of the hair will have its own colour, the intermediate colour. The top and belly colours are important

because the colour of the hair tip is obviously the most visible. The various top and belly colours are described in the colouring descriptions.

Intermediate and base colour
The previous section makes it clear what is meant by intermediate and base colour. These colours can be revealed by blowing into the coat. The hairs lie back, forming a kind of rosette that clearly shows the base, intermediate and topcoat colours.

Body condition and care
In this section the standard says, 'The Guinea Pig must feel strong and muscular, meaty but not fat or thin, and free of tangles and damage. The eyes must be clear and sparkle with vitality. Nails should not be too long, and should

be clipped as necessary, so that they are flush with the foot pad. Soles of the feet, nails and the outside and inside of the ears must be clean. The animal must not be visibly pregnant, and must be free of any diseases or parasites.'

It should be made clear here that Guinea Pigs sold in pet shops are not pedigree Guinea Pigs. After all, they've been bred as pets, and not for showing. You could call them 'mixed' Guinea Pigs, but they're often the nicest and most good-natured pets.

Still, it's worth finding out how close your pet Guinea Pigs come to meeting the standard. Some parts of the standard relate to things like body condition and

care, which can be applied to any animal, pure bred or ordinary pet. So, you can look at your Guinea Pigs through the eyes of a show judge: are they not too thin, or too fat? Is their coat well looked-after?

Sheltie

A longhaired Guinea Pig's coat is at its best at an age of 9 to 13 months.

It would be going too far to describe all the breeds, colourings and markings of the Guinea Pig in this book. After all, that's what the breed standard is for.

To give you some idea about the colourful and varied world of the Guinea Pig, this chapter gives a brief overview of a number of breeds, colourings and markings.

Breeds

There are presently nine recognised breeds of Guinea Pig. These are distinguished mainly by their coat structure. The most common breed is the Smooth-haired.

The Coronet Guinea Pig is also smooth-haired but has a crest of fur on its forehead.

The Shorthaired has an irregular coat that feels stiff.

There are three varieties of longhaired Guinea Pig. The Peruvian is the best known. This variety has two rosettes on its hind body. The Sheltie does not have these rosettes. The Coronet wears a crest of fur as a 'crown' on its forehead.

The Satin is a new breed. The hairs of this smooth-haired Guinea Pig are hollow, giving the coat a satin gloss. The coat of a Rex is like that of a teddy bear. The Tessel is a cross between a Rex and a Sheltie. It has a curly coat and very dense hair.

Colourings

A colouring is a group of colours that belong together. There are two main groups of colourings: the agoutis and the single-coloured

varieties, called 'selfs'.
Agouti is a speckled colouring, but also a natural colouring that occurs in the wild. The speckling comes about because the hairs have a tip of a colour different to the rest (usually black). Guinea Pig enthusiasts refer to this as 'ticking' or 'wild colour pattern'. Agouti Guinea Pigs come in the following colourings: Gold Agouti (warm chestnut), Gold (red with black ticking), Grey Agouti (chamois yellow with black ticking, also called wild colouring), Silver Agouti (silver-grey with black ticking), Cinnamon Agouti (silver-white with cinnamon ticking), Salmon Agouti (soft orange with dark grey ticking).

The self colourings all have just a single colour. The following colours are recognised: Black, Chocolate (dark brown), Lilac (bluish with a reddish glow), Beige (dark crème colour with a grey shimmer), Red (warm chestnut red), Gold (warm orange), Buff (dark yellow-ochre), Crème (light cream colour) and White. A White Guinea Pig may have red or dark (brown or blue) eyes.

Markings

A marking is a fixed colour pattern. There are various recognised markings. It can be very difficult to breed the separations between the colours exactly where they should be. The Brindle is a marking where two colours must be equally distributed over the whole body. The

Tortoiseshell is a complicated marking. Several sharply segregated fields of colour are spread over both sides of the body, and a clear parting runs along the ridge of the back. The colour fields must be rectangular and are only recognised in the red and black colours.

The Japanese is also red with black, but the colours here are in bands around the body and head. The segregation between the colours runs from front to back along the middle of the back and belly. Where the left half of the body is red, the right half must be black. The red side of the head must have a black ear, and vice versa. This marking is particularly difficult to breed.

The Tricolour has three colours distributed evenly across its body. The Dutch has the same marking as the Dutch rabbit (white with black fields on head and rear body). The Rus is white with a dark point around the nose, dark ears and feet.

There are many other colourings and markings that are not yet recognised, such as Dalmatians, Dappled, Stoat, Harlequins or Silver Salmon Agoutis.

Dutch

Peruvian

Tricolour

Apart from the tame Guinea Pigs we know so well, there are a number of other Cavy varieties, some of which are closely related to 'our' Guinea Pig whilst others are somewhat further removed from them.

The Wild Cavy

Because no-one knows exactly from which variety the tame Guinea Pig descended, we can't say for sure that this is its wild form. In terms of build, the Wild Cavy (*Cavia aperea*) certainly looks like the twin of the tame Guinea Pig. It sports a pretty, red-brown fur with black ticking and is less plump than the tame Guinea Pig.

Special cavy species have been kept in some zoos (including the Berlin Zoo) for some time. Breeding of the wild Cavy in captivity has had mixed success, so the population is not that big. One assumes that care and reproduction of the Wild Cavy would be identical to that of its tame counterpart.

The Yellow-toothed Cavy

The Yellow-toothed Cavy, or Cui, (*Galea musteloides*) is not so closely related to the tame Guinea Pig, and belongs to another genus (*Galea*). The Yellow-toothed Cavy is an animal that lives in groups, and is active during the day. Young are born all year round. After a pregnancy of 54 days, the mother gives birth to a litter of one to seven babies. They weigh approximately 100 g at birth and are suckled for 23 days.

Some Yellow-toothed Cavys are kept in captivity. Some years ago they were bred fairly successfully, but for some unknown reason this has stagnated. The Yellow-toothed Cavy is more slender that the real Guinea Pig. Its coat is a speckled grey in colour.

The Rock Cavy

The Rock Cavy (Kerodon rupestris) is also known as the 'Mountain Cavy' and, in contrast to other Cavy varieties, it is an excellent climber and jumper.

In the wild, Rock Cavies live in trees and along rocky slopes. They move along, balancing on thin branches. At certain times of the year, the Rock Cavy is also active at night. Females give birth to their young once or twice a year. Just like the other Cavy varieties, Rock Cavies don't require elaborate care.

The Tschudi Cavy

The Tschudi Cavy *(Cavia aperea tschudi)* is a sub-variety of the wild Cavy. Some experts regard this sub-variety as the ancestor of the tame Guinea Pig. In the wild, it lives on the slopes of the Andes mountains (central Chile), where it is found at heights of up to 4200 metres. This variety of Cavy lives mainly off grasses and herbs.

Apart from the varieties we've described above, we also know of the Dwarf Cavy (*Microcavia australis*), the Amazon Cavy (*Cavia fulgida*) and the Peruvian Cavy (*Cavia stolida*). However, these varieties are quite rare and little is known about them. They are not kept in captivity either.

Nutria

Hutia

A number of distant relatives of the Guinea Pig: Nutria, Mara, Hutia and Chinchilla

Mara

Chinchilla

If you let a male and female Guinea Pig live together, there's a very good chance you'll get additions to the family. So, before you do this, you need to be sure that you really want to start breeding Guinea Pigs.

A litter of baby Guinea Pigs is nice, but after the second or third litter, it can become difficult to find good homes for the young. So, think about reproduction (wanted or not) when you buy the animals. If you want a male and a female, but no young, you can keep them in separate cages or you can have the male castrated.

Guinea Pigs don't bear young as often as mice or hamsters. Without some form of birth control, a pair will produce a litter of two to five young a maximum of four times a year.

Male or female

It is normally not so simple to tell the difference between the sexes. You have to examine them closely, under the tail. As with most rodents, you can tell the difference by the distance between the anus and the genital opening. This distance is much greater on males than on females. On fully-grown males you can also see the shape of the scrotum.

In-breeding

A responsible breeder will never mate just any male with just any female, because of the risk of in-breeding. If you were given a brother and sister from the neighbours, it's best not to breed with them. If these animals

Breeding

produce young, this is a serious form of in-breeding, and who is to say that the neighbour's litter in turn wasn't also produced by a brother and sister?

One count of in-breeding is certainly not a disaster, but several times in succession will quickly show disastrous results. The young get smaller and weaker with each litter, fewer young are born and congenital abnormalities are likely to appear.

Mating

Wait until your Guinea Pigs are five to seven months old before breeding. At that age, the female's bones are still supple enough to be able to stretch when giving birth. Females that give birth for the first time at an older age have

it much tougher.
Guinea Pigs don't like mating in the open. They are very discreet and mate when nobody can watch. Only one mating session can take place when the sow is in season (ready to mate). Her season is accompanied by a lot of agitation within the Guinea Pig community. A sow goes into season once every 16 days for a period of a few hours. A membrane in the vagina breaks during her season, allowing mating to take place. The boar leaves a wax-like plug in the vagina to prevent sperm from flowing out.

Pregnancy and birth

Pregnant Guinea Pigs can become very fat, although sometimes you may notice nothing at all until three-quarters of the pregnancy

A shorthaired dappled-red mother with her young. The young are all red.

has passed. The Guinea Pig's pregnancy lasts some 65 to 70 days and it's a tough time for the female. Guinea Pigs are sensitive to stress, so give the mother-to-be plenty of peace and quiet. Towards the end of the pregnancy, the female is often so heavy that she can barely waddle her way around the hutch. Her body weight may increase by between 50 to 75 percent. The sow now needs extra vitamin C, so give her a 50 mg tablet daily.

The birth can usually take place in the cage. In principle, the male can be present, but the sow is ready to mate again within 24 hours after the birth, so it is best to house the male somewhere else at this time.

The birth usually goes smoothly and quickly. All the young are born within a fifteen-minute period.

When a baby is born, the mother licks open the amniotic sac and bites through the umbilical cord. Never touch the young with your bare hands as the mother will reject them because of the scent they leave behind.

Development
The reason for such a long pregnancy is that young Guinea Pigs are born fully developed, fully covered in fur and with eyes and ears open. They can even run, straight after being born. Animals born in this completely developed condition are called precocial. Because Guinea Pigs can flee from predators immediately after birth, their parents never have to build a proper nest or burrow. The young animals' stomachs are fully developed and ready for solid food, but they do take their mother's milk for about a month.

Happily, Guinea Pigs generally have few health problems. A healthy individual has bright eyes and is lively. Its coat is smooth, soft and regular (except for the shorthaired variety). Its rear body is dry and clean.

A sick Guinea Pig sits withdrawn all the time. Its coat is dull and stands open, as if wet. A sick Guinea Pig tends to be particularly listless and curls up quietly in a corner.

Prevention

The rule that 'prevention is better than a cure' also applies to small animals such as the Guinea Pig. It's not always easy to cure a sick Guinea Pig.

Even a light cold can prove fatal for a Guinea Pig and the biggest risks to its health are draughts and damp conditions.

There are a few general rules that you should follow if your Guinea Pig falls ill:

- If the animal lives together with others in the same cage, remove it as quickly as possible. It may be infectious and pose a risk to your other animals.
- Keep your animal in a quiet semi-dark place. Stress, crowding and noise won't help it get better.
- Keep your animal warm, but make sure its environment is not too hot. The best temperature is 18 to 21°C.
- Don't wait too long before visiting a vet. Guinea Pigs that get sick have little will to survive and may die within a few days.

- The patient should always have fresh water – remember that your animal may be too weak to reach its water bottle.
- Sick animals often eat little or nothing. Give it a small piece of apple or other fruit.

Colds and pneumonia

Draughts are the most common cause of respiratory problems for Guinea Pigs, so choose the place for its home carefully.

They can withstand low temperatures relatively well, but cold in combination with a draught can lead to the development of a serious disease. The first signs include sneezing and a wet nose. If the condition gets worse, the animal starts to breathe with a wheezing sound and its nose will run even more, so it's now high time to visit the vet, who can prescribe antibiotics. A Guinea Pig respiratory disease must be kept in a draught-free and warm room (18 to 21°C).

Diarrhoea

Diarrhoea is another formidable threat to Guinea Pigs and often ends fatally. Unfortunately, diarrhoea is usually the result of incorrect feeding, sometimes in combination with draughts or damp. Some cases of diarrhoea are caused by giving the animal food with too high a moisture content. Rotten food or dirty drinking water can also be a

Black

cause. You can do a lot yourself to prevent diarrhoea.

Should your Guinea Pig become a victim then you must take any moist food out of the cage immediately. Feed your animal only dry bread, boiled rice or crispbread. Replace its water with lukewarm chamomile tea. Clean out its cage litter and nest material twice a day. As soon as the patient is completely recovered, you must disinfect its cage.

Tumours

Guinea Pigs relatively often have problems with tumours, mostly in old age. Tumours occur frequently in strains where in-breeding has occurred (i.e., where animals have been crossed with members of their own family). The most common tumours are benign or malignant tumours in the skin, but they can also affect the female's teats. These forms can be operated on but, because of the animal's age, this rarely makes sense.

Another cause of lumps in the skin is an abscess. This usually starts with the penetration of the skin by a grass seed or similar, or perhaps a bite. An abscess can be treated easily by the vet, who opens and cleans it. Should your Guinea Pig show signs of a tumour, take it straight to the vet's. Delay will only make things worse, both with skin cancer and abscesses.

Broken bones

Guinea Pigs sometimes break bones because they get stuck with their paws, jump from your hand or arms, or fall from a table. An animal with a broken paw will not put weight on it and will limp around the cage.

If it's a 'straight' fracture (the limb is not deformed), this will heal within a few weeks. Take care that the Guinea Pig can reach its food and drink without difficulty. In the case of a serious fracture such as a broken back, it's best to have the animal put to sleep. If in doubt about a possible fracture, always see your vet.

Teeth malformations

Guinea Pigs that are fed a diet with too few minerals run the risk of developing broken teeth. If you notice that your Guinea Pig has a broken tooth, check that its diet is properly balanced. The vet can prescribe medications to restore the calcium level. A broken front tooth will normally grow back, but you should check regularly that this is happening.

A Guinea Pig's front teeth grow continuously and are ground down regularly by its gnawing. A genetic defect, a heavy blow, or lack of gnawing opportunities can disrupt this process. Its teeth are ground down irregularly and in the end don't fit together properly. In some cases the teeth continue to grow

Texel red

Texel red-white

Texel black

Flea

Mite

unchecked, even into the opposite jaw. When a Guinea Pig's teeth are too long, it can no longer chew properly and the animal will lose weight and eventually starve to death.

Long teeth can easily be cut back. A vet can show you how to do that, or do it for you if you don't feel up to the task yourself. Make sure that your rodent always has enough to gnaw on. A piece of breezeblock, a block of wood, or a branch will do fine.

Parasites

Parasites are small creatures that live at the expense of their host. The best known are fleas on dogs and cats. Guinea Pigs seldom have problems with parasites, and healthy animals certainly don't. Weak, sick or poorly cared for animals, however, are far more likely to be affected. Generally, you discover parasites only when an animal starts to scratch itself and develops bald patches. If you notice that your Guinea Pig is itching and scratches itself frequently, then it's probably suffering from lice (tiny spiders that feed on blood). Such lice are often spread by birds. A pet shop or vet can give you advice on how to deal with parasites.

Fleas

The most common kind of flea found on Guinea Pigs are cat fleas. Guinea Pigs are not especially vulnerable to them. If your other pets (especially cats and dogs) are free of fleas, then your Guinea Pig will rarely have problems with them. But if your cat does suffer from fleas, then these will often jump to your Guinea Pig. If you're treating another pet for fleas, then don't forget your Guinea Pig(s). They are best treated with flea powder or spray. Make sure during treatment that your Guinea Pig won't be able to breathe it in.

Skin mites

The skin mite is a particularly harmful parasite. Fortunately they seldom occur, but if they do affect your Guinea Pig, you've got your work cut out for you! Mite infestations by a form of sarcoptic mite causes intense irritation, resulting in serious self-mutilation, hair loss, scabs and infections. Insecticidal dusting powder is effective if given early, but severe infestations need veterinary attention.

Ear mites or mange

If your Guinea Pig frequently shakes its head or holds it tilted, there's a good chance it's suffering from ear mites (or mange), which is also caused by tiny parasites. They feed on the surface of the skin inside the ear. The continuous irritation causes the ears to produce more wax, so that the whole ear fills with filth, which results in heavy itching. You can diagnose ear mites by simply looking into the ear. Your vet can prescribe ear drops and a cleaner, which will clear the problem quite fast.

Worms

A Guinea Pig can also suffer from a number of internal parasites. These are tiny organisms that live inside its body. Almost all parasites are specific to one animal type only, so be careful when introducing new animals as they may bring worms with them. Treat all new animals for parasites before allowing them to mix with your original Guinea Pigs.

A Guinea Pig with a worm infection may not become seriously ill at once, but will lose weight and be more vulnerable to other diseases.

Fungal skin infections

Guinea Pigs can sometimes suffer from fungal skin infections (ringworm) which leave tiny flakes of skin around their ears and nose. These infections are easily spread both to other animals and humans, but they can be treated. Don't let such infections go on too long, because they can lead to all kinds of other problems. Your vet has good treatments for fungal infections.

Deficiency ailments

The importance of sufficient vitamin C has been mentioned several times in this book. A shortage of vitamin C is the most common deficiency ailment suffered by Guinea Pigs. However, other deficiencies can also lead to disease. The accompanying table gives an overview of the diseases that can be caused by certain deficiencies.

Old age

Obviously we hope that your pet will grow old without disease and pain. However, Guinea Pigs live nowhere near as long as humans and you must reckon with the fact that after just a few years you have an old Guinea Pig to care for. Such an old Guinea Pig will slowly become quieter and get grey hair in its coat – and now it needs a different kind of care. The time for wild games is over; it won't like them any more. Leave your Guinea Pig in peace. In the last few weeks and days of its life, you will notice its fur decaying and the animal will get thinner. Don't try to force it to eat if it doesn't want to; the end is usually not long off. Guinea Pigs, on average, live about five years. A seven-year old Guinea Pig is very old, but in exceptional cases they can reach an age of eight years.

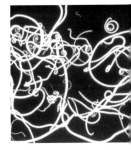

Roundworms

Tapeworms

Deficiency of	Symptoms	Found in
Protein	Poor coat, hair loss, pneumonia, infertility and poor growth of young animals, aggression (both with too much and too little)	Peas, beans, soya, cheese
Vitamin A	Pneumonia, damage to mucous membrane or eyes, growth problems, diarrhoea and general infections, cramps, small litters	Root vegetables, egg-yolk, fresh greens, bananas and other fruit, cheese
Vitamin B complex	Hair loss, reduced fertility, weight loss, trembling, nervous symptoms, anaemia, infections	Oat flakes, greens, fruit, clover, dog biscuits, grains
Vitamin C	The Guinea Pig can't produce vitamin C. Deficiency results in bad growth, disturbance of the immunity system, internal bleedings, lameness, decreasing fertility	Fresh greens and fruit
Vitamin D	Growth problems, poor bone condition Too much vitamin D causes calcium loss in bones and calcium deposits in blood vessels	Dairy products, egg-yolk
Vitamin E	Infertility, muscle infections, nervous problems, bleeding and poor growth of young animals	Egg-yolk, sprouting grains, fresh grains, greens
Vitamin K	(Nose) bleeding, poor healing of wounds and growth problems. Normally produced in the animal's intestines.	Greens
Calcium	Lameness, calcium loss in bones and broken teeth	Mineral preparations, dairy products, sepia, varied diet
Potassium	Weight loss, heart problems and ascitis, wetness in open abdominal cavity	Fruit
Sodium	Can only occur with serious diarrhoea	Cheese, varied diet
Magnesium	Restlessness, irritability, cramps, diarrhoea and hair loss	Greens, grains
Iron	Anaemia, stomach and intestinal disorders, infertility	Greens, grains, meat
Iodine	Metabolic disorders and thyroid gland abnormalities	Greens, grains, water

- A Guinea Pig is NOT a pig!

- Never leave an animal in a car parked in the full sun.

- Draughts are a Guinea Pig's biggest enemy.

- Visit a small-animal show. It's worth the effort.

- Hay is an important food for Guinea Pigs. You can give it unlimited quantities.

- If a Guinea Pig is eating poorly and dribbles, check its teeth.

- Guinea Pigs and small rabbits can easily be kept together.

- Buy your Guinea Pig from a good pet shop, or from a good breeder.

- Vitamin C is vital for a Guinea Pig's health. It needs it every day.

- Children will be children. Don't let them play with an animal unsupervised.

- Don't buy a Guinea Pig that's too young – but not too old either.

- Think before you act. Buying an animal needs careful consideration.

- Guinea Pigs must always be kept free from frost.

- Guinea Pigs are social animals and need company.

- Prevent large variations in temperature.

Tips

Becoming a member of a club can be very useful for good advice and interesting activities.

Southern Cavy Club
www.vivamiga.u-net.com/

Northern Cavy Fanciers
www.freewebs.com/northerncavy/

Cavies Galore, a guinea pig community
http://caviesgalore.com/

The Scottish National Cavy Club
www.members.lycos.co.uk/
scottishcavies/

Kent Coast Cavy Club
www.stelling-minnis.co.uk/
kent-coast-cavy-club.htm

Addresses

Name:	Guinea Pig or Cavy
Latin name:	*Cavia aperea porcellus*
Origin:	Large areas of South America
Male:	Boar
Female:	Sow
Body length:	24 - 30 cm
Weight:	Boar: 1.1 - 1.8 kg
	Sow: 0.8 - 1.5 kg
Number of teats:	2
Heart rate:	230 - 370/minute
Breathing rate:	100 - 150/minute
Body temperature:	37.5 - 39.5°C
Sexual maturity:	Boar: 3 months
	Sow: 5 months
Season cycle:	16 days
Length of season:	20 - 24 hours
Gestation:	65 - 70 days
Number of young:	2 - 5
Weight at birth:	50 - 145 g
Suckling period:	4 weeks
Life expectancy:	Average 5 - 7 years (maximum 8)